Dedication

To my two beautiful daughters.
May your light always shine

The Adventure of Little Bean
Copyright © 2021 by Ageno H Monica
All rights reserved. This book or any portion there of may not be reproduced or used in any manner whatsoever without the express written permission of the publisher except for the use of brief quotations in a book review.

Printed in Melbourne, Australia

First Printing, 2021

ISBN: 9780645287851

Kingdom Books
Melbourne, Victoria.
3166

The Adventure of
Little Bean

By Ageno H Monica

Once upon a time, when Little Bean was just a seed, he was dropped in a hole in the road. It was not a very good place to land, but some rain fell on him and he began to grow.

He opened his little bean arms and stretched out his little bean leaves. 'Oh dear!' cried Little Bean, when he realised that he was growing in the middle of the road.

'I cannot put my young roots down in the middle of the road. The ground is too hard for them to grow!'

Mr. Caterpillar happened to pass by
and he asked Little Bean, 'What are you doing
in the middle of the road? It is only a matter of time
before a car runs you over.'
'Oh dear!' cried Little Bean, 'Can you please
help me find a new home?'
'Follow me,' said Mr. Caterpillar, 'I think I know
just the place for a new home.'

So Little Bean dug himself out of his hole
and he and Mr. Caterpillar crossed the road.
Mr. Caterpillar found a corner at the side of the road.
'This should do us just nicely. This gutter will make
us a beautiful, new home.'
However the pavement was too hard for Little Bean's
roots to grow through.
'Mr. Caterpillar, this cannot be my new home,' said Little
Bean, but Mr. Caterpillar did not hear him.
He was tired and had already rolled himself into
a ball and gone to sleep.

Little Bean was upset that he had not found
a new home, so he continued his search.
Mr. Frog came across Little Bean
and asked him, 'Why are you looking sad?'
'I want to find a new home, but the pavement
is too hard for my roots,' said Little Bean.
'You need a swamp with soft soil
and water,' said Mr. Frog.
'That sounds really wonderful,' said Little Bean.
'I can take you there,' said Mr. Frog.
So little Bean followed Mr. Frog to the swamp.

'This is it!' said Mr. Frog as they
reached the swamp. 'This is a beautiful home
that will do us nicely.'
Little Bean looked around at the swamp.
The water was very dirty and full of chemicals.
Little Bean sank his roots into the mud,
but it was so bad that it began to make him sick.

'This is not a good home for me,' cried Little Bean, but Mr. Frog did not hear him. He had already jumped into the water and swum away.

Still feeling very sad, Little Bean kept searching for a home.

Miss. Bluebird landed beside Little Bean and asked him, 'Why are you so sad?'
'I cannot find a new home,' he replied.
'The road has too many cars, the pavement is too hard and the swamp is too dirty.'
'In some places humans pour their chemicals and rubbish into the water and this makes it bad for little plants like you,' said Miss. Bluebird.
'I know a clean place where you can grow.'

So Miss. Bluebird carried Little Bean away from the city and planted him beside a clean stream of water. 'This will do just nicely,' said Miss. Bluebird.

'Yes it will!' cried Little Bean happily
as he sank his roots into the soft soil.
Little Bean was so happy with his beautiful new home.

The water was clean, the soil was soft
and the air was fresh.
Soon Little Bean grew to be a big, happy Bean Stalk.

LESSON:

Take good care of the environment so that plants like Little Bean can have a home to grow and be strong just like you.

Do you know what plants like Little Bean need to GROW?

Clean water

Sun light and fresh air

Good soil

HOW CAN YOU HELP KEEP THE ENVIRONMENT A GOOD PLACE FOR PLANTS LIKE LITTLE BEAN?

Pick up rubbish near you and put them in a bin

Put plastics in the recycle bin

From The Author

I Write books because I believe in the importance of reading to children from an early age.
I hope that my books can engage and teach children values that build their confidence

I love to hear from my readers, connect with me at
agenomonica.com
and signup for our fun filled mailing list.

Find me on
facebook @ www.facebook.com/Ag.H.Monica
instagram @agenohmonica

Would you mind taking a few minutes to leave a review of my book? It is important because your opinion helps people to make better decisions
thanks!

Ageno H Monica

Made in the USA
Middletown, DE
11 March 2024